# Goodbye Miss Maisie

INSPIRED BY A TRUE STORY

DR. RUDY MENDOZA

Copyright © 2021 Dr. Rudy Mendoza

## Goodbye Miss Maisie

All rights reserved. No part of this publication may be reproduced, distributed, or transmitted in any form or by any means, including photocopying, recording, or other electronic or mechanical methods, without the prior written permission of the publisher, except in the case of brief quotations embodied in critical reviews and certain other noncommercial uses permitted by copyright law. For permission requests, write to the publisher, addressed "Attention: Permissions Coordinator," at info@beyondpublishing.net

Quantity sales special discounts are available on quantity purchases by corporations, associations, and others. For details, contact the publisher at the address above.

Orders by U.S. trade bookstores and wholesalers. Email info@ BeyondPublishing.net

The Beyond Publishing Speakers Bureau can bring authors to your live event. For more information or to book an event contact the Beyond Publishing Speakers Bureau speak@BeyondPublishing.net

The Author can be reached directly at BeyondPublishing.net

Manufactured and printed in the United States of America distributed globally by BeyondPublishing.net

New York | Los Angeles | London | Sydney

ISBN: 978-1-637920-16-9

# DEDICATION

To my lovely eternal companion and queen, Theresa, who captured my heart and imagination, invigorating my senses, always serenely and wisely reminding me the worth of a soul is eternal.

# TABLE OF CONTENTS

Prologue .................................................................................. 7

Chapter 1: Welcome to Bluebonnet, Pre-K to 6th Grade .. 9

Chapter 2: Ramona 1985 ......................................................... 13

Chapter 3: Rueben 1951 ........................................................... 21

Chapter 4: Silverio 1990 ........................................................... 29

Chapter 5: Adina 1991 .............................................................. 35

Chapter 6: Timothy 1995 ......................................................... 43

Chapter 7: Matilda 1998 ........................................................... 51

Chapter 8: Cody 2001 ............................................................... 59

Chapter 9: Juan 2005 ................................................................ 65

Chapter 10: Luis 2008 ............................................................... 71

Chapter 11: Maribelle 2012 ..................................................... 77

Chapter 12: Cynthia 2015 ........................................................ 83

Chapter 13: Lucas 2016 ............................................................ 89

Chapter 14: Miss Maisie 2020 ................................................. 95

# PROLOGUE

There was not a person Maisie did not teach.

*Goodbye, Miss Maisie* was born out of a desire to tell the story of a teacher, and the impact a teacher has on the world around her.

Everyone grew up with a Miss Maisie in their life. She is everything we remember – a good teacher, an educator who seems to know exactly what a student needs for social-emotional support and growth, and able to deliver that in a way that is kind, subtle, and thoughtful. Miss Maisie loved every one of us deeply. I never knew how that was possible.

Miss Maisie taught her way into all sorts of classrooms at multiple learning levels, dealing with myriad life situations, and handling it all with inspiration and tact. She never regarded the color of a child's skin, nor whether they were rich or poor. She only saw their soul.

*Goodbye, Miss Maisie* is a story for teachers looking to feel the appreciation that they richly deserve. In this new age of education, it is a reminder for us why so many decided the classroom was where we would live out our lives.

It is true that we had many wonderful teachers over our lifetime. Most of us had only one Miss Maisie.

CHAPTER 1

# WELCOME TO BLUEBONNET, PRE-K TO 6TH GRADE

Bluebonnet Elementary is like most antiquated urban elementary schools. Constructed in the early 40s of the last century, it is a spacious building situated on a large lot. Because of its size, the school serves students from pre-kindergarten to sixth grade. Yet, in spite of its size—or perhaps because of it—it also has several portables set aside to meet the needs of the large, diverse student population.

Upon entering the school, a visitor captures both the history and modern flairs that make this building unique. Recent bond proposals aggregated a new two-story section that included a library, as well as office space and classrooms. An elongated hallway encased by windows to see outside links the new building to the old one. The vintage portion of the school is comprised of two wings for classrooms, the cafeteria, gymnasium, and auditorium.

Due to a recent bond approval, the entire school was being repainted, retiled, and repaired where time and attention had played a role in aging the building. As you walk the hallways and visit the classrooms, the smell of freshly splashed paint permeates the air. Within the new portion of the building, you notice new furniture—steel-framed chairs with attached desks, clean whiteboards, and new wooden cabinets ready to be filled with student backpacks and display student work.

Conversely, as you travel through the old portion of the building, you notice cracks within the walls in the hallways and in the classrooms. Unfortunately, the bond allocations only included paint for these areas that had become stressed over time. Although these classrooms have similar tools used for instruction found within the new portion, the original buildings' resources are clearly weathered. Vintage wooden tables and chair-desks are marked by the many students who passed the time creatively drawing or practicing their writing skills on said surfaces. In some cases, crib notes that could have been used for a multiplication test are teased out. These tables and chairs are also off-centered and vary in size and height. Over time and extensive use, these whiteboards are less white, yet still serve their purpose. Instead of cubby spaces for backpacks, students have access to antiquated lockers lined up along the hallways just outside the classrooms.

In spite of its contrasting design, Bluebonnet has a unique character that is often the case where attention to student learning exists. Although there is a clear delineation between modern and vintage amenities, such as water faucets, the air conditioning system, and the public announcement system, a distinct school spirit and pride is evident where portraits of past principals served line the main corridor, as well as student trophies that have been acquired over the years, representing academics and the fine arts accolades.

Both the school and the neighborhood have seen better days. During its inception, Bluebonnet ES was surrounded by a vibrant and budding neighborhood. Early on, it was a predominantly Anglo-Saxon Jewish community. Over the years, as a result of desegregation and other factors related to city growth and zoning, the school became increasingly diverse.

The school is located near the periphery of a bustling and economically thriving downtown. Although it is within minutes of upscale shopping and neighborhoods, this small part of the world differs with dilapidated buildings and in some cases abandoned homes that surround it.

Over time, the school demographics transitioned from predominately white to African-American. Currently, the majority student body is represented by a large Latino population comprised of mostly immigrants from Mexico and multigenerational Mexican-Americans. Still, diversity does exist with a smaller percentage of African-Americans and Anglo students in attendance. Even

though the student body may be racially and linguistically diverse, the majority of the student body shares commonality in the area of income generated by their parents.

Every day, for hundreds of children, it was home.

CHAPTER 2

# RAMONA 1985

The class arrived promptly at 7:50 a.m., as this was the first day of school. This was also Miss Maisie's first day as a teacher in charge of her own classroom. The cool September light fell in through the window, onto the hard linoleum floor. Parents hurried with backpacks of all the colors on the color spectrum, something waiting for these kindergartners to surely learn about in the nine months they would be in this classroom.

Their fearless leader, Miss Maisie, sat in a chair at the front of the room. On the chalkboard was written in big, beautiful cursive, "Welcome, kindergartners! Your life awaits..." Miss Maisie waited for the parents to get their children calmed down, settled in, and ready to go. Her dark brown hair fell gently over her ears, her cool glasses signaled to the parents that she had a life outside the classroom, but her big smile reassured them that this is what she lived for.

There was always a wide variety of ways kids reacted to their first day of kindergarten. There were those who begged their parents, tooth and nail, not to leave them with this strange woman in this strange place. This was Ramona, who with her bright, blue eyes and confident haircut looked like someone who ought to be able to handle something this simple. But beneath her proud look was a scared little girl, who had no idea what waited for her in this classroom.

Then of course, there were the outgoing students. The kindergartners who seemed to say, "I got this" while they walked around introducing themselves to the other students, as if they were at some networking event or cocktail party. One such student was Julia, who looked over at Ramona and her parents with quiet bemusement. *What is her problem,* she thought to herself, while moving towards the Legos with her brave new friend, Antonia. "Do you know that girl", she asked Antonia. "No but she is really crying," Antonia noticed.

Ramona's parents brought her into the consolation of Miss Maisie, who assured her all would be fine. With their guts in a knot, Ramona's parents left for the door, and left their daughter to her new life and the loving, instructive care of Miss Maisie. Ramona immediately liked Miss Maisie. There was something warm and natural about her presence that made her immediately trustworthy. Miss Maisie scanned the room and brought the class to attention.

"Welcome, kindergartners. I am your teacher, Miss Maisie."

"Hello, Ms. Maisie," the class boomed back in unison.

"Now to start the day, we are going to each get a partner. Your partner is going to trace your hand on a piece of paper, and then, you are going to write your family members on it . This will be turned into me, so I can go home and get to know each of you a little more."

"Can I be with Antonia!?" Julia shot up from the corner of the room.

"Why don't you be with Ramona here," said Miss Maisie, in her infinite wisdom.

Julia slunked to the front of the class. "Hi, I'm Julia," she said to her doe-eyed new partner.

"I'm Ramona," Ramona replied.

"You want to go do this?" Julia asked, compassionately. Ramona nodded her head. Julia could tell that she was sad, and reached for her hand. "Come on, let's go".

Julia carefully traced Ramona's hand on a clean sheet of cardboard. "Wow, I love your nail polish."

"Thanks," said Ramona. "Okay, your turn." Ramona took her new friend's hand and gently placed it on her sheet of cardboard. "What is your favorite color?" asked Ramona.

"Purple," said Julia. Ramona looked for the purple marker.

"That was nice of you to ask," said Julia, "I'm sorry I didn't ask you." "It's okay," said Ramona, "I like all the colors."

When the day finally ended, and the parents came to pick their students up, Ramona seemed to have recovered from her morning. Ms. Maisie looked on, proud of her new students. After the morning activity, Julia had taken Ramona by the hand and introduced her to all of the friends she had made.

Ramona was excited about her new class, and couldn't stop talking about it in the back seat on the car ride home.

"Do you like Ms. Maisie?" her dad asked.

"Yeah, she seems nice," said Ramona. Ramona's parents looked at each other and gave a knowing look. Some kind of magic had happened in that classroom, and they knew Ms. Maisie was behind it.

Fall turned into winter, and winter into spring, and when the first signs of summer were afoot, the final day of kindergarten came, and the class sat eager to hear their final words of wisdom from Ms. Maisie. Ms. Maisie had done her job well. She knew every one of her students. She had spent a precious moment with each of them. They had learned about the color spectrum, and they had learned to spell, and above all, they had learned what it means to be in a community of learners, friends, and fellow kindergartners. She watched the rambunctious lot talkative on the learning mat which they had come to call home.

"Okay, everyone," Ms. Maisie said, and she pulled out a stack of cardboard from her drawer.

"Remember these?" Miss Maisie showed them the stack of palm prints they had done the fall before.

"Yes!" the students said, amazed to see this relic of archeology unearthed.

"So, here is what we are going to do, to celebrate the last day of school. Please take your partner's cardboard handprint, and write a message on the back for your partner, to take with them into the new year." She called up each of the partners from that first day's activity and handed them their friend's hand print. When she said, "Julia", Ramona had a shiver down her spine. Julia took Ramona's cardboard sheet, and wrote, "Never be afraid to say hello! You are the best." Ramona was called up, and she took Julia's sheet of cardboard. She considered for a while the message she would write on the back, but she decided to say, "Keep being a great friend! Love, Ramona." They exchanged their sheets and smiled at each other.

Julia looked at Ramona after she handed her the cardboard. She felt such a sense of care for her friend, she said, "Remember the first day of school? When you were so scared."

"Yeah, I was," said Ramona, "I am so glad that Miss Maisie made us partners." "Me too," said Julia. They both looked at Miss Maisie, helping a boy in their class spell "love". They would miss their teacher. "Okay, everyone," said Miss Maisie, " when you are finished, please bring these to your parents when they pick you up! And please gather back on the learning mat when you are finished."

Ms. Maisie looked at the assembly of young people gathered on the floor. She looked at Ramona and Julia. She welled up with tears. Ramona and Julia sat next to each other, holding hands. With their friendship, Ramona had made friends with so many of the kids in her class. And everyone had seen Julia be nice to Ramona that first day, and because of that, all the kids would always go to Julia when they got sad. She wondered what would have happened, had she not paired the two of them together on that first day. Would Ramona have continued to be scared and not like school? Would Julia have continued to be mean to students she just didn't understand? She felt happy for their friendship, and knew it would carry them well into the first grade.

The students sat anxiously awaiting their final words from Miss Maisie, before being released to the freedom of the summer. "Thank you all for being the most wonderful kindergarten class. I will miss you all so much. I want you each to go around and say one thing that you learned this year."

And soon, the orchestra began. "Sharks", "Coloring", "Numbers", "Friendship", "Asking for help", "Counting", "Decorating"...the list went on and on, and Miss Maisie saw not a group of kindergartners, but a collection of young people beginning to learn about themselves and the world around them. And she knew that they were beginning to see themselves that way, too.

The bell rang, and parents began to flood the classroom, ready to collect their kids for the summer adventures ahead. "Bye, Ms. Maisie," they each said one by one. Ramona ran up to give her a hug as she got to the door. "Bye, Ms. Maisie," she said, quietly tearing up.

"Goodbye, Ramona. You are going to make a great first grader".

## CHAPTER 3

# REUBEN 1988

Miss Maisie welcomed the first grade class like she does with all her classes: a big smile, concerned eyes, and an excitement that is palpable. Miss Maisie always has recess duty in the first grade, because that is where so much learning really happens. Cliques are made, alliances formed, hearts are broken, knees are scraped. Life happens on the playground, and the rules of the inside do not always follow the students out into the adventure land of the jungle gyms and swings.

The imagination gets to run wild in the playground at recess, and Miss Maisie could almost see the playground become a world of lava and volcanoes, of castles and of football fields. She could hear the fans cheering when someone scored a goal, and she could hear the clicking of the medical equipment in the makeshift hospital rooms, or the babies crying that were being nursed. Lives were spelled out in the playground, words were spelled out in the classroom, and Ms. Maisie lived to be able to be there for both. The mostly quiet, guiding force that she was.

One student, Reuben, always hit the playground with levels of enthusiasm unseen by even Olympic gold medalists. He would hit the blacktop and charge, screaming at the

top of his lungs. Who knew where he would end up today, but every day, he would return to the classroom sad, defeated, and morose with eyes that said, "Why me, Miss Maisie?" Miss Maisie was spending more time looking at Reuben and trying to learn about what it was exactly that was causing him so much trouble. He would start out every day high as a kite, and would end recess with the wind out of his sails.

One particularly sunny Tuesday, Miss Maisie made it her mission to determine what it was that was happening out there between the swings and the slide. Was it a bully that she didn't know about? Was it that Reuben is a sore loser, something she had encountered many times before in the first grade boys that she had an easy time of correcting. This was Miss Maisie's personal mystery, and she was committed to solving the case.

She watched as Reuben started the jam-packed twenty minutes of recess. He ran immediately to a group of older kids playing four square.

"Can I play?" asked Reuben.

"Sure," they said.

She watched Reuben play with amazing skill, getting his older opponents out. She saw the sparkle of a young humility, he wouldn't take a bow, he would just say thanks for letting me play, and move on to another game on the playground.

He approached a group of girls – which was bold, but understandable – and he asked them what they were doing.

"We are playing doctor," they informed him.

"What is wrong with her," he asked of the young patient, who lay motionless with her hands across her chest on the ground.

"She had a bad day," said the lead physician, a girl named Eliza.

"Oh no," said Reuben, "Can I help?" "Yes, that would be great." Eliza handed Reuben three large pinecones from one of the protective pines that swooped over this field of imagination. "These are special medicines. If you put them on her heart, she will feel a lot better." Reuben did as he was directed, and the girl began to cough little. Then, miraculously, she got up.

"I feel so much better," said the girl, "thank you." "No problem," said Reuben, "I am happy to help."

There was still at least ten minutes of recess left, and Reuben didn't know what to do. He looked left, and there were some boys digging a hole, for God knows what reason. He looked right, and there was a very spirited game of chase going on. Neither of them seemed that fun to him, so he went to the wall of the school and sat down in a slump. He put his head in his knees and began to cry.

Miss Maisie, of course, saw all of this. She walked over to him and put her hand on his shoulder.

"Reuben," she asked. Reuben looked up from tear-soaked eyes.

"Hi, Miss Maisie." He gave a good sniffle and then sat more upright—after all, this was his teacher.

"Why are you here?" Reuben asked.

Miss Maisie gave a warm smile. "I saw you playing and then you walked over here all by yourself, and I was wondering what happened?"

Reuben started to tear up again, touched by her compassion, and gave her a knowing look. "I just don't know what to do, I don't want to play any of the games that everyone else is playing." "It seemed like you were having a lot of fun playing doctor with Eliza, and playing four square with the older boys." Reuben was amazed she had seen all that. Miss Maisie did have an incredible way of knowing exactly what was happening.

"You saw all that?" asked Reuben, tearing up again.

"Yeah, and everyone seemed so happy to have you there with them."

"Yeah, I guess," said Reuben.

"What would you rather be doing?" asked Miss Maisie.

The thought hadn't crossed Reuben's mind. He always thought of recess as a time to do what other kids were already doing. "I don't know," he answered. "Well, you know you can make up your own games, too."

The school bell rang, and everyone rushed to enjoy the last seconds of recess, before hurrying back into line and into their afternoon classes. Miss Maisie gave Reuben her hand. "Come on," she said, and walked with him into the classroom.

They sat down, and Miss Maisie began the afternoon lesson. She was talking about whales, but all Reuben could think of were the games or activities that he could be doing on the playground. He dreamed of being a pirate and captaining a crew. He dreamed of being an explorer, or of building a railroad. All this time he had been playing other kids' games because he wanted to fit in, and every time he had been left disappointed. Maybe Miss Maisie was right, maybe he could make up his own games. He looked up to her at the front of the classroom. He had completely lost whatever she was teaching about now, but it didn't really matter—he had learned something much deeper today.

The next day at recess, Reuben walked slowly onto the blacktop. He looked cautiously around. His legs were shaking a little bit in his socks. What would kids think of him, off doing his own thing? Kids would think that he was weird, or strange, or worse, that he didn't like them. Eliza waved to him, from over where another operation was about to take place. One of the cool older kids gestured for him to come over and play. Reuben smiled and shook his head. He wanted to be an explorer today, and he was going to do that no matter what. He wanted to find treasures on the playground and begin to build his treasure chest. He walked over by himself to the grassy edge of the playground, and with his nose to the grass, he began combing it for what he might find.

Miss Maisie, of course, watched all of this from her station. *What is Reuben doing*, she wondered. But it was different, and she took that as a good sign. She watched Julia, from across the playground, see Reuben wandering with his nose to the brush.

She started to walk over to him. "Hey, what are you doing?" she asked him. "I am exploring," said Reuben, with laser focus on the ground before him.

"Can I help?" asked Julia.

"Sure," said Reuben.

They scoured the ground in silence, when Julia exclaimed, "Look at this!" She held a big, shiny quartz crystal.

All of the other kids heard Julia's ubiquitously loud voice, and saw she was holding something in her hand. "I wonder what that is," one of the young doctors said, and they abandoned their operation to go find out.

"Wow, that is so cool," Reuben said, studying Julia's treasure.

As the year went on, Miss Maisie watched Reuben's team of explorers transform into pirates, Robinhoods, scientists, geologists, birdwatchers, and all kinds of amazing games. Reuben would come back from recess supercharged for the rest of the day.

"Hi, Miss Maisie" he would always say, as he went out for another day of recess. Which, Miss Maisie knew, really meant, "Thank you."

When the last day of school came, and the last recess bell rang, Reuben walked up to Miss Maisie. "Goodbye, Miss Maisie," he said, "thank you for being the best teacher." "Thank you, Reuben," she said, "for being the most independent young man." Reuben gave her a big hug, and hurried inside. There was still a whole new year of recess to come, and he looked forward to the adventures it would hold.

CHAPTER 4

# SILVERIO 1990

"Silverio! Do you know how much I love your name?"

Silverio was one of Miss Maisie's quietest students. He was intellectually brilliant. In spite of having recently moved from Mexico, he was acquiring English at a quick clip. At least he was able to communicate well in his second language with his friends outside playing at recess. He was equally capable of mixing his Spanglish – that English and Spanish mixture – while eating meals prepared by his mom in the cafeteria visiting with his friends.

In the classroom, Silverio's confidence level was slowly blossoming as he continuously transitioned between his native Spanish language to his newly adopted English language. Still, he was naturally reticent to open up to all of his classmates, so he cautiously engaged with Miss Maisie. His infectious smile and warm disposition made it easy: he truly relished the opportunity to learn new things!

His dad had worked hard for many years to save enough money so that he could bring his family to the U.S. After laboring in construction jobs and any other job he could get, Mr. Ramirez was able to send for his wife and children. Silverio was the oldest boy and had two younger sisters. This was his first year in an American school and was struggling not only with learning a new language, but also with adapting to a new school culture.

Miss Maisie took an immediate interest in ensuring that Silverio felt welcome in his new surroundings. Making each student feel welcomed and cared for was her way. She established a partner or buddy system within her classroom to encourage building up a community of young learners who would assist each other in sharing their learning and understanding of the material for the day. The bilingual pairs also allowed students to interact with each other beyond classroom learning as students became friends, sharing in their young experiences. Miss Maisie always knew what to do.

As the months passed, Silverio's academic prowess grew by leaps and bounds. Although he was growing confidently in English and learning the ropes of what it was to attend his American school, he remained reserved. Miss Maisie knew only that he, like many of her students and most of the students who attended Bluebonnet, came from a humble home with parents working tirelessly to provide the essentials for their growing family.

It was late November, and the spirit that filled Bluebonnet resonated with holiday festivities that had recently transitioned from Thanksgiving and was in full sway of preparing for Christmas break. Primary classrooms were filled with hand-shaped turkeys, while the upper grades had displays of the first Thanksgiving on display. For most, there was a jubilant fever in the air as everyone anticipated the well-deserved winter break that would provide a time of rejoicing, celebration, and family unity.

However, for Silverio, this time of the year would be very different from others. Mr. Ramirez had recently lost his job. A recent recession hit his work very hard such that he was let go. Mr. Ramirez and his family turned to family members who lived nearby. Unfortunately, the only shelter an aunt was able to provide was the dingey, musty attic. So, for the last month-and-a-half, Silverio and his family were living in a dilapidated room that had no electricity. That meant no heat for the coming winter months, which translated to no running hot water. Miss Maisie could tell something was going on with her student long before she heard the knew. The combined families living under one roof with almost no food and certainly no warm clothes for Silverio and his younger sisters was tragic. Miss Maisie asked Silverio one day after class, "Silverio, why have you been down recently?"

All it took was him being asked to have his eyes well up with tears, and he ran to Miss Maisie for a hug. "I'm sorry it's been so hard," Miss Maisie said, embracing him. As she was hugging Silverio and he was crying, Miss Maisie's wheels were already turning. She would see what the school and community could do to help this young family.

When Silverio left, Miss Maisie went to her computer, and began to type an email, "Dear Principal Soliz, it has come to my attention that..." and so, she spelled out the plight of the Ramirez Family. She coordinated with the Principal and PTA members, and she reached out to other colleagues who she knew had influence and resources. They feverishly collaborated to determine who might provide to support Silverio and his family.

It took a few weeks, but on the last eve before winter break, Miss Maisie and a small coalition presented the Ramirez family with a bundle of gifts that were gathered to help and support a family in need. Miss Maisie was able to connect the family with social services that allowed them to access electricity through a payment plan. This meant no more cold showers! It also meant that the humble house would be filled with warm air, instead of the cold and clammy air that left a chill to the bone.

Miss Masie reached into the gift bag and pulled out an almost brand new winter coat. "I think that this one has your name on it, Silverio," she said. They had also provided donated winter clothes that included sweaters, long pants, socks, and even gloves and hats. Silverio would no longer be walking to school in his shorts and polo shirt. Now, he had pants that matched the school uniform, as well as sweaters that he could use for layers. He smiled, "Thanks, Miss Maisie."

The collective effort spearheaded by Miss Maisie resulted in the Ramirez family being able to store their food cabinets with both dry canned goods as well as some homemade dishes: tacos, enchiladas, and caldo de res to name just a few. Miss Maisie thought of them eating a warm meal as she sat down on the sofa with her relatives to enjoy her winter holiday. It made her feel better knowing that Silverio was having a good night, too.

The Ramirez family was overwhelmed with joy and deeply appreciative of the care given by their community, their school, and their teacher – Miss Maisie. They felt welcomed, and part of a community that would catch you when a big wind knocked you off the ladder.

Upon returning from winter break, Miss Maisie was called into the principal's office, where she was handed a letter written by Silverio. Because Mr. Ramirez was unable to find any employment, he determined that it would be best to return to their native home in Mexico, where he and his family would remain until economic conditions improved. "Goodbye, Miss Maisie," it said in handwriting far beyond what was age appropriate, "you'll always be my favorite teacher."

Silverio wanted Miss Maisie to know how much he appreciated all that she did for him as his teacher, but also for what she did for his family. Miss Maisie wiped the tears from her cheek and thanked the principal. This was the part of teaching that always broke off a piece of her heart. Maisie returned to the classroom where her children were waiting for her.

# CHAPTER 5

# ADINA 1991

"Adina, can you please try that again?" Miss Maisie asked, her warm eyes looking down at the very challenging second grade math problem facing Adina. Adina looked up, her eyes fierce with concentration. She was determined to figure this math problem out. Adina looked up at Miss Maisie.

"Maybe if you'd taught me better, I'd be able to do it," she coldly said.

This wasn't Miss Maisie's first rodeo, she knew that this kind of frustration and anger could lead Adina to say things she didn't really mean deep down. This is how it was with anyone and everyone. Miss Maisie quietly said, "If you haven't learned how to do this, then we'd better pay some extra special attention." Adina got quiet, and scooted over in her chair to let Miss Maisie get a closer look at what she was confronted with.

Adina wasn't alway this frustrated and upset in school. In first grade, she had been the star of her class. She had built the greatest Lego sculptures, and she had won first place in the field day three-legged race. Beyond all of this, she had always looked out for the other students. She knew when someone was being mean. She had been congratulated on always sticking up for people and doing the right thing. She had done fine in math, but

the problems were a lot easier than the ones that she had now. Multiplication was what they were learning, and there were not enough popsicle sticks in the world to help her understand what everyone else knew so well.

This was the piece that upset Adina the most, and Miss Maisie could tell. She worried for her, not feeling a part of the class, and she could see the terrible consequences that would follow if she got left behind. Adina was jabbing her pencil onto her paper when the final school bell rang. Adina looked up at Miss Maisie with a look that seemed to say, "Now what?"

"I tell you what, Adina. Why don't you go home and tell your parents that I am going to meet you before class to give you a little extra help on this project. Why don't you come to school an hour early? Do you think you can wake up that early?" Adina hated this idea, but she knew it was what she had to do. Moreover, she was moved that Miss Maisie cared enough to do this. It meant she was going to be getting up an hour early, too. "Deal?" asked Miss Maisie.

"Deal," said Adina.

Adina went home that night and was restless. What would she have to do to learn what she needed to learn? What if she never learned? She looked up at the ceiling in dread. Tomorrow couldn't come soon enough, and she hoped that it never would come. She looked out the window. The snow was gently falling on the street below. She watched older folks walking arm in arm, and she thought about them—they all probably knew how to do what she couldn't do. She was the worst, she thought, she'd never grow up.

When sleep finally came for Adina, all she dreamed about was gigantic multiplication monsters, who were trying to eat her. Then, Miss Maisie would come, scold them like she sometimes did, and they curled up and became like puppies. She invited Adina up to pet them, which she did—cautiously, of course—only to find these multiplication monsters reveal to her the secret of what she needed to do to master them. Sadly, she awoke early to not remember anything at all about what she was supposed to do!

She ran downstairs and found a bowl of cereal waiting for her. Her mom was up in the other room, she could hear her. She quietly sat down at the table, and with sleep in her eyes, she began to eat. *It is so cold and dark outside, it might as well be bedtime,* she thought.

"Good morning, sweetheart," she heard her mom call from the other room. Of course, Adina didn't say anything; she was nervous and focused on the task at hand: cereal.

When she finally made it to school, the halls were deserted. There was none of the usual laughter and running and jumping that made school, well, school. She could hear the echo of her footsteps as she approached Ms. Maisie's room, backpack on and ready to learn. She opened the door and saw Ms. Maisie sitting at one of the low tables, ready for her. She had two blank sheets of paper, a ton of colored pencils, and a large cup of coffee. Or at least Adina thought it was coffee.

"Good morning, Ms. Maisie," Adina said, politely. "Good morning, Adina. How are you feeling this morning?"

"Tired," said Adina, as she sat down at the table and gave out a big sigh.

Ms. Maisie smiled and looked at her. "Are you ready to learn this? I am going to do whatever it takes, so that you do, so you can just sit back and relax."

Adina looked at her teacher with such loving, tender eyes. "Thank you," she softly spoke.

"Of course, Adina. It is my pleasure. So let's start with this."

She handed Adina a pencil. "I know you like to draw, so I think this will be a lot easier and more fun if we make it colorful."

"Thanks," said Adina, taking the pencil back into her hand.

"So," said Ms. Maisie, "when was the last time you saw a group of things?" Adina thought back in her mind. There were the monsters in her dream, but she couldn't remember how many there were exactly. She thought back further, she remembered the window and the street covered in the light of the streetlamp and the falling snow, and the young people walking down the street arm in arm. "I remember seeing groups of people walking down the street last night."

"Great," said Ms. Maisie, "why don't you draw them, but remember to draw exactly how many people were in each group.

Adina took her time with this. She drew the house, and she drew the street. Then, she drew the street lamp and the falling snow. Finally, she drew three groups of two young people each.

"How many people are on the street?" asked Ms. Maisie. Adina counted them one by one. "Six," she said.

"Right," said Ms. Maisie, "and how many are in each group?" "Two," said Adina.

"Right, so if there are three groups of two people each, and there are six people total, what is two times three?" "Six!?" said Adina.

"Exactly," said Ms. Maisie, "I think you're gonna get this quickly."

The next week, the students got back their multiplication test. Ms. Maisie called everyone up to the front of the room as they were leaving school. Adina watched the other students lead the way, nervous about what she would soon find out. Adina was called last. Ms. Maisie looked her in the eye, "Good job," she said quietly.

"Thank you," whispered Adina. She looked back at the other students, who were reading over their graded tests. Ms. Maisie said with her eyes, "Go sit down." "Okay class, I am going to say goodbye now and wish you a fabulous winter break." "Goodbye, Ms. Maisie," they said in cheerful unison.

Adina woke up early the next morning, but not as early as when she had gone to see Ms. Maisie. She walked sleepily down the stairs and into the kitchen. The light was beginning to shine in through the window, glowing on the snow-capped houses that lit up her small block. On the table, as always, was a bowl of cereal and a glass of milk. Adina poured the cereal and began to eat. *What a crazy last week of school,* she thought. She was so excited to just kick back and watch TV. *I want some orange juice,* she thought. She walked up to the fridge. There, pinned to the door, was her test. It read, 9/10, A, for Adina.

Adina started to well up with tears. Her mom walked into the kitchen and saw her daughter standing there. "Is everything okay, Adina?"

"Yeah," said Adina, "everything is great."

"Good," said her mom. "Your dad and I are so proud of you; you should be proud of yourself, too." "I am," said Adina, "and now I just want to watch some TV." "You can do that," said her mom, smiling.

Adina spent the rest of the day watching TV, but she couldn't help but do multiplication—or as she called it, times—in her head while watching the shows. Three groups of pokemon and their trainers meant six characters total. Five stalls with three horses each meant fifteen horses. She could add up the groups. She wished a little that she could turn off her brain, but she thought of Miss Maisie. It was like she was there watching TV with her, which she loved.

CHAPTER 6

# TIMOTHY 1995

Timothy always had a million things on his mind, on his plate, on the floor of his bedroom, and in Ms. Maisie's third grade classroom. Let's take a short inventory: twenty-seven Legos, three temporary tattoos, a lunchbox, an apple juice, a change of shorts, some rocks from the recent geology field trip, his special crystal, a feather he ground on the playground, a note from his friend Alladin, a picture of his older sister, a binder that was falling apart and used to house a few of these things—all of this was spread out like a fortune teller's cards on the floor of the classroom.

Kids would be tripping over his odds and ends. "Timothy!" they would yell, "Clean that up." Timothy would take a few of his wayward objects and do something like cleaning up, but usually he would just move the mess a few feet to the left or the right.

One day, when Ms. Maisie had them making holiday wreaths, Timothy managed to get pine needles down his pants. He leapt up and began scratching his butt, trying to get those pesky things out of there. This, of course, set off jeers of laughter amongst his fellow third graders, and even a bit of taunting. One boy quipped the name, "Mess Timmy", which, of course, made Timothy burst out in tears, run for the door with his pine-needle rash, slam the door closed, and start to bawl in the hallway. Ms. Maisie stepped outside and put her hand on Timothy's shoulder.

"Timothy," Ms. Maisie said, but Timothy was inconsolable.

"Why am I so messy?" Timothy said through the tears.

"I don't know, Timothy," said Ms. Maisie. She was stumped. How would she help him without forcing him into a habit that he'd bristle against?

"I just like all my things so much. I like to have them around." "I know," said Miss Maisie, "I know."

When Timothy had calmed down, he and Miss Maisie walked back inside. "There will be no referring to Timothy as anything other than Timmy or Timothy, are we clear, class?"

"Yes, Miss Maisie."

The few times Miss Maisie did have to be stern, the class fell into line with her quickly. They respected her, deep down, and craved her approval. This was because they knew how much Miss Maisie really cared about them. She went on, "We each have different skills and talents, and we all have things that we need to work on. This class is about learning how to support and encourage one another. Are we clear?"

The chorus resounded, "Yes, Miss Maisie."

Anthony helped Timothy finish his wreath, and they were delighted and smiling by the end of class. Timothy left school that day feeling alright—or so it seemed to Miss Maisie—but Miss Maisie was troubled. How could she help Timothy without singling him out and embarrassing him?

She would have to think that one over. It was still on her mind as Miss Maisie drove back to her house, through the snow-covered fields and around the wide bend, to where her little house stood proud. She always liked to sit back after a long day, return emails and texts to friends, or watch a good mystery show. Miss Maisie was on her way to doing all this, as she was taking off her jewelry and placing it in the special box her grandmother had given her. *Isn't this just the most marvelous box?* she thought. And then, it dawned on her.

The next Monday at school seemed like any other day to all of the children as they piled in to Ms. Maisie's third grade classroom. Ms. Maisie watched as Timothy got to his desk and began to unload all of the contents in his backpack onto the desk in one great, heaping pile. Kids were discussing the details of their weekend, complaining about being back at school, of course. One particularly charming girl had brought banana bread that she baked the night before, which Miss Maisie had hidden until snack time. Amidst all of this, nobody seemed to notice the beautiful pinewood boxes that Miss Maisie had at the front of the class, or the pile of paints and newspapers and magazines for cutting and collaging.

"We are going to do something fun today, inspired by this," said Miss Maisie, pulling out her grandmother's antique jewelry box. "This was given to me by my grandmother, and I love this box so much, it just makes me want to keep my things in it." The kids were all amazed by the little box, and soon were diving into making their own special boxes. Timothy, of course, made a gigantic mess, but soon took time and energy to make this box the greatest thing he'd ever made. He picked out his favorite magazine clippings from National Geographic and pasted them on to the side of the box. He had hippos and mountains from the Himalayas, he had some of his favorite words— "play" and "light"— pasted around it, too. When the lunch bell rang, Timothy felt he had created something spectacular. But he didn't know what to do with it.

"What should I do with my box, Miss Maisie?"

"I don't know, Timothy. Why don't you think about how it could help you the most?"

"I'll think about it at lunch," said Timothy. "Goodbye, Miss Maisie." "Bye,

Timothy, have a nice lunch."

Timothy ate his lunch on the playground with some other boys, who were all talking about their favorite sports teams. Timothy's mind drifted to other things—all of his things, to be exact. He thought not about the cucumber sandwich his mom packed him (which he loathed) or the Jets or the Giants; he thought about his plethora of things back there in the classroom, and his new thing: the box. It would be so hard to carry everything, with the box now, too. He heard the lunch bell ring, signaling that it was time for them to return to Miss Maisie's class.

When he entered the classroom, he saw all of his friends searching for things to put into their boxes. No one could find much. His friend Anthony only had his favorite coloring book and some pencils. Eliza only had a stapler her dad gave her. Timothy felt bad for all of them, not having things to put into their boxes. He looked at his heap of things, his treasures, and he selected his favorite sea shell, and walked over to Eliza. "Here you go, you should put this in your treasure box."

"Wow," said Eliza, "thank you."

"Of course," said Timothy.

He looked over to his friend Anthony, who had his hand in the back of his desk, searching for something that might be back there, other than stuck on gum. "Anthony, here," said Timothy, "take this!" And Timothy handed him his favorite purple crystal. It felt good to help other people fill up their boxes, and it made Timothy feel like he had a fresh box and could begin to fill it up with the new treasures he would find.

As the school year dragged on, Timothy's Treasure Box became something like an additional classmate. Even Miss Maisie referred to it as "Timothy's Box", and if a student needed, say, a glue stick, and all of the ones in the class were being used, Miss Maisie would say, "Go ask Timothy if he has something in his box for you."

As Timothy's collection grew within the box, he began to have a clear inventory of what he had and what he needed. He even asked his parents for specific things for the holidays, to help bulk up areas of his box he felt he lacked. Everyone appreciated Timothy's special box, especially Timothy, who was no longer losing things constantly. And now that everyone else had a special box, Timothy would bring his recess treasures - a feather or an errant piece of candy - and see that Ophelia's box was looking a little thin.

"Here you go, Ophelia, take this," Timothy would say. As the end of the year approached, Timothy didn't know what to do with his box. He didn't want to drag it all the

way upstairs for the fourth grade class. And anyway, the box had things that a third rader would need, like glitter glue. As the students poured out of Miss Maisie's class on the last day, Timothy stayed behind, holding on to his box.

"What are you going to do with it?" asked Miss Maisie. Timothy looked up at his teacher.

"I think you should have it," said Timothy, "for next year's class." "I think they will love that, Timothy," said Miss Maisie, "why don't we find a special spot in the corner of the classroom to leave it. But here," Miss Maisie pulled out a Sharpie marker, "we need to write your name on it." In her beautiful cursive, she wrote, *Timothy's Treasure Box*. "Now, all the students will know that it was you who left it here for them."

Timothy welled up with tears, "Bye Miss Maisie, I will miss you."

"Bye, Timothy, I will miss you too." They hugged goodbye, and Timothy gave one last fleeting glance to the box that had housed all of his treasures.

CHAPTER 7

# MATILDA 1998

Matilda was an exemplary fourth grade student. She was neat; she was organized. She was far and away the brightest fourth grader Miss Maisie had. She would never say that, of course, but her and Matilda had a special kind of affinity. Matilda would be asked by Miss Maisie to help the other students with spelling, math, and science. Matilda, of course, never noticed that this was Miss Maisie's special way of acknowledging her gifts and talents. Matilda was shy. If other kids decided they wanted to take her toy, or wanted her to do their homework for them, she had a hard time saying no. Miss Maisie noticed this, along with everything else.

One particular day, Miss Maisie noticed Matilda was picking at her food in the lunchroom. "Why aren't you eating?" asked Miss Maisie. Matilda just shrugged and looked gloomily at her hot dog. She had eaten some of the sweet corn and the slice of bread. But she poked the hot dog like it was a cat sleepily pawing at its least favorite toy. "Matilda," Miss Maisie said, "I need you to be well-fed, because this afternoon, we are going on a field trip." "I'll be fine," Matilda reassured Miss Maisie.

"Okay," said Miss Maisie, "the bus is leaving in fifteen minutes." Matilda just nodded her head.

The students piled onto the bus, one by one. There was always a certain electricity that accompanied any school bus field trip. There were infinite amounts of shenanigans that students could get into. Matilda knew all this; so did Miss Maisie. Perhaps they were the only two who were resolved to sit quietly and wait for the bus to arrive at its destination. In this case, they were going to meet with a group of opera singers, who were going to show the students what it takes to be an opera singer. Matilda was excited—she loved singing—but she worried about the other students and how they would probably find some way of embarrassing the whole class. She would always cringe whenever that happened, and wished she was in the fifth grade, at least.

They piled off the bus and into the dimly lit auditorium where they were going to experience all the sights and thrills of the opera. They were asked by a booming voice overhead to please take their seat. Matilda picked a seat right next to Miss Maisie, and they watched as the lights dimmed and the stage was illuminated.

A strange, short man with a snoutlike nose said, "Welcome, fourth grade class. We are thrilled to introduce you to the delights of the opera." Miss Maisie looked at Matilda and smiled. Matilda seemed to be nodding back in her chair, ready for a nap.

"Is everything okay?" asked Miss Maisie.

"I guess I'm just a little hungry," whispered a weary Matilda.

As the performance went on, Miss Maisie could tell Matilda was growing more and more irritable. She wished she had a granola bar or something to give her. She wished even more to know why it was that she was not eating her

lunch. Maybe something was going on at home that she didn't know about? Maybe she just doesn't like hot dogs? This was something she'd been noticing for a few days now. She nudged Matilda awake.

Matilda looked up as a beautiful woman began to speak about the qualities of a great opera singer. "A great opera singer needs to be assertive, without being harsh or mean. Sort of like in life." Matilda saw Miss Maisie smile; Matilda wondered what she meant. The singer let out a great big bellow of a note that about blasted Matilda out of her seat.

"Woah," said Matilda.

Matilda was passed out asleep on Miss Maisie's shoulder for the whole bus ride back to the school. Miss Maisie gently shook her awake when they arrived at the parking lot, so as to not embarrass her in front of the other kids.

"We're here?" asked Matilda sleepily.

"Yes," said Miss Maisie.

"Okay, bye Miss Maisie."

"Bye, Matilda." Miss Maisie handed her the backpack that she knew Matilda would meticulously load and unload every single night. "See you tomorrow, Matilda."

The next day at school, in addition to the normal lesson plan, Miss Maisie was committed to discovering just what it was that was keeping Matilda from eating lunch. She needed Matilda to have her full marbles in the afternoon; she was, in a way, her little assistant. Miss Maisie decided to eat lunch in the cafeteria that day, and sat next to Matilda. Matilda was poking at what looked like beef stroganoff.

"Not your favorite meal?" asked Miss Maisie.

"I am a vegetarian," said Matilda.

"Oh, that is wonderful. How did I not know that?" asked Miss Maisie, warmly.

"Yeah, the old lunch lady knew, but the new lunch lady doesn't." answered Matilda.

"Well, why don't you tell her?" asked Miss Maisie.

"I don't want to make her upset, I don't know," said Matilda. "I just freeze up in line and she slaps this on my plate, instead of extra other stuff, like what the old lunch lady did."

"Well Matilda, all you need to do is speak up and tell her. I am sure she will be happy to accommodate you," Miss Maisie reassured her.

"Well, what if the kids behind me in line get mad at me for holding up the line?" Matilda asked, dissecting the beef stroganoff in front of her.

"Well, then those are kids who will have a lot of problems in life, waiting in lines, won't they?"

Matilda smiled a little, but didn't let up her pensive gaze, "I'll think about it. But why can't you just tell her for me?"

"Because it is your body and your lunch, Matilda, and you need to learn to always speak up and advocate for that. Sadly, I won't always be with you," said Miss Maisie, which she could tell struck a quiver of sadness in Matilda.

"I know," she said.

The next day in line, Matilda awaited the fatal moment when she would be confronted with the lunch lady. The lunch lady was stout, and she never smiled. Her hair was pulled back in a hairnet, but wild strands flung out left and right, which Matilda always imagined finding its way into her food. She bristled with that awful thought. Matilda picked up the cold, blue tray that would come to house her next meal. She heard a group of boys behind her laughing. *At me, probably,* she thought. Everything moved so quickly in this corral of a lunch line. How would she ever be able to say what she needed to say to the lunch lady? She felt the shuffle of feet push her closer to where the scoops of food were being laid out on plates.

She got up closer to the lunch lady. "Excuse me," Matilda said, in a mouse's voice. The lunch lady looked at her and scooped the regular serving of meat onto her plate. Matilda paused; she became paralyzed. She was defeated, her face falling.

"Is everything okay?" asked the lunch lady.

Matilda briskly nodded and hurried out of the line. Miss Maisie saw Matilda exit and sit down with her plate of food. She was getting her mashed potatoes wet with tears. Miss Maisie walked over, and without saying a word, took her plate. "I'll eat this one.

You go in there and try again. Remember what the opera singer said: you can be firm and assertive, and still be polite. Channel her. You got this." Matilda looked up in awe, and rose from her seat.

"Okay, I'll try." She got back in line. Miss Maisie watched her straighten up and take a deep breath. She disappeared into the line.

Then, out of nowhere, Miss Maisie heard something between a loud shout and singing, "I am a vegetarian!" She smiled to herself. Maybe not the most graceful, but it would do the trick. Matilda returned to the table and was blushing. "She said I have such a pretty voice," said Matilda.

"You do," said Miss Maisie, "and next time, you don't even need to do that to be able to get your point across. People want to listen to you, Matilda."

Matilda had plenty of energy in the afternoons from there on out. Miss Maisie noticed she was able to say no to boys who wanted her to do the brunt end of their school work. She watched Matilda even stand up for a girl who was being picked on. When the school year came to a close, Matilda walked up to Miss Maisie. "I just wanted to say goodbye, Miss Maisie. Thank you for telling me that I could use my voice."

"You'll need it in fifth grade," said Miss Maisie.

"I got this for you," said Matilda. It was a CD of Aerosmith.

"I like his voice," said Matilda.

"I will check it out," said Miss Maisie, "we all need to be assertive sometimes."

## CHAPTER 8

## CODY 2001

"Dear Miss Maisie," the letter began, "Please forgive me for not being good in class today.

Sincerely, Cody." Miss Maisie read the chicken scratch. She couldn't for the life of her think of what it was that Cody did wrong. Cody wasn't that much of a troublemaker. Sure, he would make the occasional joke, but whatever he did to write this kind of letter and then leave it with her discreetly at the end of the school day, Miss Maisie simply had no idea whatsoever what could have gone wrong. Miss Maisie resigned herself to having to wait until the next morning to ask Cody what had happened.

The students of the fifth grade class came pouring in, like they did every morning. Miss Maisie was there ready for them, lesson plan in hand, everything she needed to get the day off to a good start. "What are we going to learn about today?" asked one particularly eager student, Jaqueline. "Today, we are going to learn about cloud formations for science, and that is what we will start with."

Miss Maisie passed out sheets of paper with different cloud formations drawn on them. Once every student had theirs, she turned on the projector and displayed awe-inspiring videos of clouds shifting in the desert sky. All of the students were gripped in their chairs, watching the cumulus clouds dance through the sky. All except for Cody, who sat at his desk with his head down, as if in shame. *Poor Cody,* thought Miss Maisie, *I wonder what happened.* As the day wore on, Cody only seemed to be doing worse. The things that all the other students found exhilarating, Cody met with a resigned remorse.

"Cody," Miss Maisie said at the beginning of afternoon recess, "can I talk to you for a moment?" Cody froze in terror. His eyes looked like he had just seen a ghost, and his face went pale. He nodded and stood as the students exited past him, into the hallway and onto the playground. "Cody," began Miss Maisie, "I received your letter, but I have to tell you, I don't know what it is about, but I appreciate something difficult must have happened." Cody stood there in terror and gently nodded. "Would you like to talk about it?" asked Miss Maisie. Cody again gently nodded. "Well, let's sit down then."

Miss Maisie and Cody sat at her desk, watching the other children play on the playground. "Looks fun, doesn't it?" said Miss Maisie. Cody gave another nod. "So, Cody," asked Miss Maisie, "what made you decide to write me that note?"

"Something happened," said Cody. "Something at school?" asked Miss Maisie. "Yes," said Cody.

"Well, what part of the day did it happen in?" asked Miss Maisie. "During lunch," said Cody.

"Was it in the lunchroom?" asked

Miss Maisie. Cody shook his head no. "Was it in the bathroom?" Cody shook his head yes. Miss Maisie was getting closer, but she really didn't know how she would be involved. "So what happened first?" asked Miss Maisie.

Like wildfire, everything poured out. "Julio was in the bathroom and I splashed him with water to just have fun, and then he got mad and said that he was going to tell you." Miss Maisie's heart broke—this was so precious—but she knew that she had to take his feelings of shame seriously. "Well, Cody, he didn't, but I'm glad you did, because now, it gives us a chance to talk about it."

"So tell me why you decided to do what you decided to do?" said Miss Maisie. "I don't know," said Cody, "I guess I just wanted to have a little fun."

"But Julio didn't think you were wanting to have fun?"

"No," said Cody, "he thought that I was pranking him."

"Did you tell Julio that you were just trying to play?" asked Miss Maisie. Cody shook his head no. "Why didn't you say that?" asked Miss Maisie.

"I guess I thought he wouldn't believe me. And I felt really bad," answered Cody.

"Is that the only way you felt, bad?" probed Miss Maisie.

"I guess I also felt sad," said Cody. Miss Maisie had hit the nail on the head.

"Well, Cody, it is good to feel bad when we violate someone's personal space, and when we do something that makes someone else feel uncomfortable. But always the person to apologize to is the person we hurt, not the person we think will get us in trouble."

Cody nodded. "And it is okay to feel sad and also feel bad. We have complex feelings as human beings, and I bet if you told Cody you were sorry for doing what you did, and were also sad he didn't want to play with you, he would understand." Cody again nodded. "Now, go out there, before recess is over."

Miss Maisie sat back and thought about how intense and complex the lives of her students were, watching the kids play on the playground. Though to adults like her, their issues were minor and petty, to them, their issues encompassed the whole world. She thought about how important it was for her to remember that as a teacher, and to do what she could to make sure her students understood that she felt that way about them. That made it easier for them to open up to her about what was going on in their own lives, and to trust her to give them feedback that took them seriously. "Bless their little hearts," said Miss Maisie out loud, as the students piled back into the classroom.

Cody and Julio walked side by side. They weren't exactly holding hands, but they did seem to have just returned from a very serious conversation. Cody smiled at Miss Maisie from across the room. Miss Maisie smiled back, and returned to the afternoon lessons. When it came time to pick partners for the game of telephone in Spanish class, Julio walked over to Cody.

"Partners?" he asked.

Cody nodded, shyly. As the day slowly came to a close, and Julio and Cody walked out together, Miss Maisie imagined other ways that the day could have gone. What if she had gotten upset at Cody for splashing water on Julio? Then, he would have been burdened with even more guilt, and quickly would have fallen deeper into his despair. It was a blessing that they were able to make up, but it took Cody getting comfortable with having a complex set of feelings. *Important life lessons for anyone,* thought Miss Maisie, in her signature dash of humility.

Cody and Julio became closer as the year went by. As the final weeks of school were approaching, Miss Maisie noticed one day that Cody was waiting for the other students to leave at the end of the school day. Once everyone had filed out, Cody was standing at Miss Maisie's desk, with a beaming smile.

"Guess what Julio did in the bathroom today?" said Cody.

"What?" asked Miss Maisie, warmly.

"Splashed me with water," said Cody with enthusiasm.

"Did you splash him back?" asked Miss Maisie.

"Only a little," said Cody slyly, "bye Miss Maisie."

"Bye, Cody. I'm glad that all got worked out."

Miss Maisie watched the energetic fifth grader walk out of her classroom. The door closed, revealing a room full of empty tables and chairs where there was previously all the life that encompasses fifth grade. Miss Maisie thought about Cody, and then thought about every other student in her class. Each and every one of them had a similar experience, a similar set of difficult emotions to work through, complex feelings to navigate. This little classroom was the canvas in which it all happened. She felt proud to be the person who made sure it was a place that could hold all of their little lives. It was, for her, so much more than a classroom. It was a cocoon, a space of infinite dreaming and possibility.

She thought again about what she needed to do to prepare for the day tomorrow. She knew that her students had no idea how much time and effort she put into class every day, but it didn't matter, because they were the ingredient she needed the most to make it a success. Their little community would march on, changing lives. *I hope that they save some of their splashing for the water balloon fight on field day,* thought Miss Maisie, as she smiled and locked up her classroom for the night.

# CHAPTER 9

## JUAN 2005

Juan was the most difficult student Miss Maisie ever had, and because of that, she loved him even more.

Juan was always in your face, screaming at you. He was a very challenging student, and for some reason, that made Miss Maisie love him even more passionately. She poured so much into her relationship with him; it became so deep. Miss Maisie could be stern, but it was because beneath that sternness a deep compassion shown that students would take to her and slowly let their pain fall away.

Miss Maisie knew that Juan must be in a lot of pain for him to treat her in the way that he did. She kept this knowledge secret, but it was her secret weapon. She took what she knew and applied it in loving him even more. Each day was a challenge, and then one day, everything changed.

Juan was banging his pencil on his desk. *Bang. Bang. Bang. Bang.* This was in the middle of Miss Maisie's lesson introduction. "Juan," Miss Maisie said, "will you please stop, so we can continue learning?"

"You want me to stop?" asked Juan, "No thank you." *Bang. Bang. Bang.*

Most students would be sent to the principal's office after something like this happened.

And most teachers would be the kind of teachers to send a kid to the principal. Miss Maisie had to do that now and then, of course, but she saw this as an opportunity to break through.

"Juan," said Miss Maisie, "we all want you to be a part of this class."

Juan looked around at the students. His friend Eduardo was covertly chewing some gum. He knew, in that moment, he was by far the worst student in this class. He felt that, he felt his pain and his sense of how much he hated school. Why did he hate school so much more than all of the other kids in this class? Was it because of the troubles he had at home, the gangs and illegal behavior that so many of his friends who were a little older were getting mixed up in? That certainly stressed him out a great deal. And here, amidst all of it, was Miss Maisie being nice to him. He dropped his pencil.

"Thank you," said Miss Maisie, smiling, "Juan, why don't we meet after class, and have lunch together today?"

And so began Miss Maisie and Juan's monthly luncheons. He went from screaming in her face to being one of the students she could rely on. She cut through the pain within him to his bigger self. Maisie knew he was a bright kid, bright enough to be a gang leader. One day, the conversation of gangs came up, and Miss Maisie asked him, "What is that like for you?" Juan took a big bite of his sandwich, and exhaled slowly. He began to chew, and looked down at the floor. "You don't have to answer me if it is too much for you," said Miss Maisie, empathetically. Juan continued to chew and stare at his shoelaces.

"It is really tough for me," began Juan. "I feel like I have no choice. It makes me angry every day."

"I can see how that would make you angry," said Miss Maisie, "But I want you to know that you have lots of other ways. There is a whole community here to support you." "Yeah right," said Juan, "everyone here just wants us to get out of their class, so we can go be with a different teacher."

Miss Maisie looked him square in the eye, "Do you really feel that way about me?" she asked.

"I guess not you," said Juan, "but you're different." The bell rang and it was time for class to begin.

"We'll talk more soon," said Miss Maisie, and at that moment, their story together took a surprising turn.

Miss Maisie had luncheons with Juan many times. She tried to show him another way, encouraging his brightness and intelligence, and making him feel like he could do whatever he wanted to do. As they continued to forge this relationship, and Miss Maisie was trying to show him another way, their relationship deepened. They were something like friends by the time the school year ended. When it came time for Juan to leave her class, Miss Maisie was distraught, as he was going on to the nearby high school. *What if our lunches are the only things keeping him out of trouble?* Miss Maisie shuddered at the thought. She wouldn't be able to see him after he graduated.

But then, something totally unexpected happened. Miss Maisie had her lunch schedule changed, out of the blue. This freed her up to walk up the block to the nearby high school, to still have lunch with Juan once a month. As he got older and more mature, so did his problems. High school was a whole new beast for Juan, and Miss Maisie, too. She was able to see that his problems certainly required a level of support that perhaps she couldn't give him, but also that he would be able to take the kindness he felt from her and bring that into the other areas of his life.

"Thank you, Miss Maisie," he would always say after every meeting. "Thank you so much."

Tragedy struck, however, when Maisie got the report that Juan had gone out for a car ride with some of his other cousins. They had crossed through the area where a different gang lived, and Juan was killed. That night, all Maisie could think of was the sweet boy at the luncheons. She could remember nothing of the kid who would be yelling and screaming at her. Miss Maisie wept because she missed Juan, and she hated that she couldn't save all of her students who needed help.

From that point on, a small beaming photo someone had taken of Miss Maisie and Juan after one of their famous luncheons was tacked proudly above her desk. When the new school year came, the class filled up with people from the grade below. Miss Maisie always preferred to think of her students as people, because that is what they were to each other and, that's what they would always be once they moved beyond being Miss Maisie's kids. She watched the new class funnel in, and she looked tearfully for a new Juan, someone she might love as much and as passionately.

"Who is that?" asked a bright-faced kid with glasses, pointing at the picture of Juan behind her desk.

"That is one of my favorite students," said Miss Maisie.

"Oh," said the kid, "he looks really nice."

"He is," said Miss Maisie, wiping a tear from her eye. "Alright, class," she said, "we have a lesson to begin."

## CHAPTER 10

# LUIS 2008

Luis entered into the hallway today as a seventh grader. Back in Mexico, where he had lived the year before, he had been in primaria, but here, in the United States, all the other kids had already been in middle school. This made him feel even more of an outsider. Even though he heard the occasional Spanish word—usually a bad word—tossed around in the hallways, and even though he looked just like most of the kids here, he felt a distinct sense of being an outsider. That, plus the fact that his English was nowhere near as good as his peers. He could get by okay, and he could enlist the help of one of his cousins in his class, but a distinct sense of apprehension and dread filled him as he walked through the hallways.

As Luis walked through the building, he noticed that it in many ways, it wasn't as nice as the school he had known in Guadalajara. There were some cracks within the walls in the hallways, and paint peeled along the trim of the windows. The air smelled of linoleum, and the hallway was filled with a cacophony of slamming lockers—something he wasn't used to. He scaled the lockers looking for his number. He had a small piece of paper with his locker number and combination the nice lady at the front desk had handed him.

As he walked through the hallway, he looked at everyone looking at him. *Everyone must know that I am new,* he thought to himself, as he looked at the locker numbers increase. 341, 342, 343, here he was, locker 344, right next to a pretty blonde girl who smiled at him.

"Hi," she said, "I am Eleanor."

"Hi, Eleanor, I'm Luis," he gave her a nervous smile.

"I don't recognize you from last year, are you new?" she asked.

Luis assumed she was thinking about his accent. "Yes, first day," said Luis.

"Well, nice to meet you," Eleanor slammed shut her locker and drifted into the sea of new faces. Luis felt completely alone.

Luis was fifteen minutes late to Miss Maisie's class. "I'm sorry," he said, closing the door behind him. The whole class looked up at him. They stared. Miss Maisie, of course, was prepared for this moment.

She looked at the class and said, "Class, this is Luis. He is one of our new students this year." The way she said "one of" made him feel so much better, so much relief. He wasn't alone; there must be other new students, too. He looked around, wondering where they might be. "Take a seat wherever you like, Luis," said Miss Maisie. Luis sheepishly walked to the farthest, back corner. Miss Maisie watched him sit down, with concerned eyes. "Luis," she said, "we were just about to go around the class introducing ourselves," she looked nervously down at the lesson plan she was supposed to complete today. "Why don't you start," she said warmly.

Luis timidly began to speak, "I am Luis," he said softly. Some jock dudes in the front row strained to listen. "I am from Guadalajara, but just moved here," he went on. "I am happy to be here and excited for the new class and new school year." Nobody, not even the girl sitting next to him, could hear anything that he said. Miss Maisie would have to think this one over. Maybe he was just nervous, since it was his first day of school.

Luis, however, was not just chalking this up to the first day of school. He was shy and nervous about his accent. It didn't matter that half the kids in the class spoke Spanish, nor that his English was honestly pretty good. He just felt totally out of place, and like he couldn't even communicate with the teacher in the ways that he needed to. Miss Maisie spoke Spanish, which Luis would later find out, but she saw a student who both needed to feel proud of his heritage and able to be successful in this new world. Miss Maisie devised a plan.

The next day at school, Miss Maisie decided that Luis would need to do something to help him begin to feel more integrated in the classroom. What would he need to feel more secure and comfortable here? Miss Maisie watched Luis again come into the classroom, and she worried that these days could only get worse.

"Hi Luis," she warmly said.

"Hi, Miss Maisie," he replied, giving her a warm smile.

"For today's project, I want you to be paired up with Brock." Luis looked at the tall, lanky, boy who looked like he might as well be working on the farm at lunch. Brock gave him the head raise "what's up?"

Luis felt very confused. *Why would Miss Maisie do that?* He looked like the kind of kid who wouldn't have nice things to say about people like himself. He looked over at his cousin, Eduardo, sitting in the corner. With his eyes, Luis seemed to say, "What is going on?" Eduardo just gave him a shrug. Luis shuffled off with Brock.

Brock surprised Luis, first, because he was really nice. Miss Maisie of course knew that, and that is why she paired Luis with Brock. She also knew that Brock volunteered at the English as a Second Language classes that ran after school, and that by the end of their time working together, Brock would have suggested that Luis come. Miss Maisie also knew that this was the most natural way to make Luis feel at home, rather than telling him what he needed to do. Above all else, Miss Maisie knew that she had power, she was seen as a teacher, and even though she was silly on the inside, she could hurt students, too. Luis looked over to Maisie at the end of the period, and his eyes seemed to say, "Thanks."

The next day, Miss Maisie found Luis in her class early. "Hi Miss Maisie," he said.

"Hi Luis," said Miss Maisie, "can I help you with something?" "I just wanted to say thank you for introducing me to Brock. He is really great." said Luis.

"I thought you two might get along!" said Miss Maisie.

"Yeah," said Luis, "he's cool." As the day went on, Luis did a lot of laughing working with Brock on his project.

He was in the middle of cracking up when Miss Maisie introduced the new class project. "Class, I want to let you all know what we will be doing next week," began Miss Maisie. "We will be doing a presentation about the project you are making with your partner. This is a separate assignment, as you will be asked to give a five to ten-minute speech about the topic you and your partner researched. You can appoint one of you to do the speaking, but both of you should contribute to writing it." Luis pointed at Brock as soon as he heard. "You," he said. But Brock just shook his head no.

The next day after class, Brock and Luis walked through the hallway. They walked toward the classroom where the ESL classes happened, through the same halls which only two weeks earlier had filled Luis with a sense of anxiety and fear. Now, he felt like his new home was emerging within these very same halls. As they were walking to the classroom, Luis asked Brock why he wanted to even help kids out like this.

Brock smiled at Luis, "Miss Maisie suggested that I'd like doing it. I really do. And plus, my mom works until six, so I like to hang out at school anyways. I don't have time to do sports, because I have to help my dad out on the weekends."

Luis just nodded, "Well, I'm glad that you decided to. I like being friends." "Me too," said Brock. "You're super cool."

When it came time for Brock and Luis to present on Mesopotamia, they were ready to go. Luis read his lines before the class confidently and proudly. Though he was shaking in his boots a little bit, he was clearly audible, even to the jocks—who, at this point, had drifted toward the back of the class, no longer trying to make a good first impression. Everyone went into a round of applause when Luis finished. Luis blushed, and tears welled up in his eyes. "Gracias," said Luis.

"Good work, Luis," said his cousin, Eduardo. "You did really good."

CHAPTER 11

# MARIBELLE 2012

Maribelle was fourteen years old. She had a little dog named Chico, whom she loved dearly.

After school, Maribelle would rush home. She would go through the gang-infested side streets to take a shortcut, sometimes nodding at one of her cousins hanging out behind a dumpster. She would walk over the trash-littered streets and make her way slowly to her little house where her grandmother would always be waiting, Chico on her lap, to give her a hug and ask how school was.

"How was class today?" her grandmother would ask, "How is that Miss Maisie? She is my favorite."

"School was good," Maribelle would reply, and quickly grab on to Chico and take him for a walk.

Maribelle never ever got involved with her cousins or any of their business. She knew that they were often getting into trouble , and up to no good. But she had a special affinity in her heart for one of her older cousin's friends, who she would see around her grandmother's house sometimes when everyone in the neighborhood knew her famous cooking was afoot. One day, her cousin's friend was over, and as they were sharing stories of the school day over her grandmother's famous chilaquiles, he gave her the eye. She was old enough to know what that meant. She really did like him, though, so when he was sweet and asked if her and Chico wanted to go for a drive in his new car, and her grandmother was asleep in front of the TV, Maribelle said yes.

They drove around the neighborhood. They drove past the school where they had gone since kindergarten. Maribelle thought about all the games she played on the playground, watching the swingset and slide drift past her in the streetlights. She looked out the window longingly.

"Remember playing out there at recess?" she asked.

"Yeah, totally," her suitor replied, "really fun days." They pulled into the back parking lot of the school, and saw the headlights illuminate the schoolyard. Then, Maribelle had her first kiss, which set tingles up her spine. She loved it. And it felt good to be close to the school.

The next day at school, Maribelle couldn't stop blushing. "Are you in love or something?" her girlfriend asked her.

"No," Maribelle said, shaking her head at the lunch table and blushing more.

This prompted her girlfriends to leap up and beg her to reveal her secret. Maribelle just shook her head no more and more, until the chaos subsided. But her glow was contagious— everyone noticed. In Miss Maisie's third period science class, she was checking Maribelle's work and said, "Maribelle, que feliz," which again brought on one of Maribelle's famous rosy red blushes.

"I'll let it be your little secret, okay," Miss Maisie said warmly, continuing her tour around the classroom.

But when she got home to see her grandmother, it was a different story. "I heard that you went out for a drive with that chamaco idiota."

Maribelle blushed. What could she say? She liked him, and she wouldn't be living with her grandmother forever. "It's none of your business," said Maribelle, "I am a grown woman now." This, of course, made her grandmother laugh, and that made Maribelle cry. She ran to her room, slammed the door, and began crying.

Maribelle curled up on her bed. She looked around at the room full of relics from her past. There was a spelling bee trophy next to her favorite stuffed animal. She heard the flicker of TV from the other room. She loved her grandmother so much, but she had to be growing up, too. She looked out the window. The snow was falling on the ground. She thought about all that she had done over the last years. She felt a sense of accomplishment and also a sense of loss for something she couldn't really put her finger on. She grabbed the stuffed animal from her trophy case and cuddled it in bed. She heard Chico scratch at the door, and she opened it for him to crawl into bed with her, too.

Maribelle kept seeing her new friend, and she grew up fast. She was still the good student Miss Maisie knew and loved, and Miss Maisie was used to watching the kids, especially the girls, grow up really fast over their eighth grade year. She tried to support them as much as possible, while also keeping them focused on their studies. Over the next days, Miss Maisie noticed that Maribelle was a little more demure than usual, especially for such a beautiful spring week. Miss Maisie approached her on Thursday, and asked if she would like to hang out after school. Maribelle, of course, said yes, as she would never pass up a chance to visit with Miss Maisie after the school day, and she had a lot on her mind.

Maribelle creaked the door open at the end of the school day. Miss Maisie was sitting at her desk, grading some tests. She looked up and saw her student shyly walk in. "You wanted to see me?" asked Maribelle.

"Yes," said Miss Maisie, "it seems like you've had a lot on your mind recently, and I just wanted to check in with you and see how you were."

Just the very touch of compassion caused her to break into tears. "My abuela is dying, and I'm pregnant." "Oh, sweetie," said Miss Maisie, "come here." Miss Maisie held Maribelle as she cried and cried in the empty classroom.

"It will be okay."

That weekend, Maribelle heard a knock on the door. Chico started barking. Maribelle's grandmother breathed slowly in and out of her oxygen tube. "I'll get it," yelled Maribelle. There, at the door, was Miss Maisie. "Hi," said Maribelle, "welcome to my house." Miss Maisie stepped inside and looked around. Chico ran up and licked her leg. "That's Chico," said Maribelle, "he's eight."

"Hello, Mrs. Gonzalez," said Miss Maisie to Maribelle's grandmother. She smiled with her eyes and nodded, and went back to watching the TV.

"What's that," said Maribelle, gesturing at the bags Miss Maisie was carrying with her.

"Ingredients for chilaquiles. I heard your Grandmother's were the best, but mine are pretty good, too."

As Maribelle ate with Miss Maisie and her grandmother and her cousins, and they all laughed and shared stories, she saw so much more than just her science teacher. She saw a friend of her grandmother's, a friend of her cousins, someone who could be like an older cousin to her.

Maribelle sank into her chair and smiled. Chico begged for some food from under the table.

"Your chilaquiles are pretty good, Miss Maisie," said Maribelle, slumping back in her chair. "I'll have to teach you sometime," said Miss Maisie, "maybe over the summer."

"Sounds good,"

Maribelle smiled, and reluctantly gave Chico a small bite.

Maribelle gave birth to a healthy baby boy, and spent a lot of time with Miss Maisie that summer. By the time ninth grade rolled around, Maribelle was ready to start school and have her baby there with her. Her grandmother recovered, and seemed to have a second wind in her.

"It must be my baby," Maribelle told Miss Maisie one day as they were baking, over the summer. "She knew that I'd need the help."

"You would be able to do it on your own, too, Maribelle, you are strong," said Miss Maisie, "but now your little boy will know what the best chilaquiles taste like."

Maribelle laughed and smiled at Miss Maisie. "Yours are almost as good," she said. Miss Maisie raised her eyebrows suspiciously.

"We'll let him be the judge, when he's a little older," she replied. The baby cooed in its crib, and Maribelle and Miss Maisie cooked into the afternoon.

# CHAPTER 12

# CYNTHIA 2015

Cynthia was the sweetest child Miss Maisie ever had. Miss Maisie would watch her from her desk during naptime, and she would always be looking at the sky, counting sheep on her hands. Whatever was tasked with her, Cynthia always wanted to be the one to do it. One day, Cynthia came to school with a terrible rash on her face. "Hello, class," she announced at the beginning of the day. "Today, I was diagnosed with eczema." Everyone in the class applauded, except for Miss Maisie of course, who knew what eczema was. As she grew older, however, eczema wasn't quite what she was hoping it would turn into. It gave her none of the magical superpowers her distressed mother promised it would, in the car ride back from the doctor's office.

Cynthia was so distraught by her face that when she had an outbreak, she would call in sick. By the time the spring rolled around, Cynthia had used up all of her excused absences, and the administration had called her parents.

"Cynthia needs to come to class," said the principal. "I will personally ask Miss Maisie to direct her class to not say anything that would be hurtful to Cynthia."

Miss Maisie sat her whole class down. She saw all of her students and thought about Cynthia. She wished

that Cynthia were here today. She missed her infectious sweetness; she would always make her feel so much better. Miss Maisie recalled how earlier in the year, she had been having a particularly hard day. She usually was good about leaving any personal problems she might be having at home, so that she could give her full self to her students. This day was different, as her father had recently passed on, and she was thinking about him constantly and missing him dearly. Miss Maisie was slinking toward the lunchroom when she saw Cynthia bounding down the hallway, her messy mop of hair flapping left and right.

As if on auto-pilot, Miss Maisie asked Cynthia the standard, "Hi Cynthia, how are you?"

Cynthia responded in an alarming, booming voice, "I'm great!!!" elongating the "a" sound for added effect. It was so disarming for Miss Maisie that she almost dropped the books that she was carrying. It was like a blast of fresh air went straight through her chest and blew all her troubles away. Miss Maisie felt so much better, seeing this boundless ball of energy that was truly great.

It made her remember why she loved teaching. And now, as her eyes scanned the classroom, this dear student of hers was not among the others.

"Now we all know and love Cynthia, and do we all remember when she told us about her skin condition, called eczema?" began Miss Maisie. The class nodded in rapt attention, as if they were hearing the most important news being read. It always was a big deal when Miss Maisie sat them down like this. Miss Maisie continued, "Now Cynthia has become sad about her face condition, and she is afraid to come here to school, because she is worried that she will be made fun of.

Now, is that anything anyone here would do?" The whole class shook their heads no. "That's what I was hoping to hear," said Miss Maisie. "So, when Cynthia comes back here tomorrow, we are going to treat her with respect." The whole class nodded their head yes, and Miss Maisie thought that she had her case settled with these young learners.

The next day, Cynthia arrived kicking and screaming. Her mom was carrying her and struggling to restrain her, as her legs flailed all over the place and her voice cried out, "No!" Tears streamed down her face. The whole class sat silently, staring at the dramatic scene unfold in front of them.

Cynthia's mom almost threw her into the classroom. She looked up at Miss Maisie and exclaimed, "You deal with her!" Cynthia sat in silence, cross-legged, on the ground. No one said a word.

"Hi, Cynthia, I am glad you are back," said Catherine, quietly from her desk.

"Me too," chirped Margaret.

Soon, a cacophony of welcome backs filled the air.

"Thank you, class," said Miss Maisie, "now let's get to learning." Miss Maisie walked over to Cynthia and put her hand on her shoulder. "How are you?" she asked. Cynthia just growled and turned her head in a huff. This broke Miss Maisie's heart, as she could see the same little girl who with the same rash on her face was bounding through the hallways. Miss Maisie kneeled beside her and put her hand on Cynthia's shoulder. Miss Maisie leaned in and whispered in her ear, "It will be alright, Cynthia.

Let's just try to have one good day." It took everything in her to keep from crying, seeing this helpless student she so adored sitting on the ground and pouting.

Miss Maisie sat at her desk as her students began working on the independent project portion of their lesson. She pretended to organize papers, but in reality, all she thought about was Cynthia, who sat on the ground pouting to herself. *What can I possibly do to help her?* she wondered. She thought maybe they could make masks as a class, but that would only make her feel worse. Abruptly, Miss Maisie stood up. The class turned, wondering what would happen next. And in front of Cynthia, she began.

"Dear Class, I want us to take a moment to acknowledge how brave Cynthia was to come here today. As you all know, we have thought about her every day she has been absent and have been hoping this day would come, when her sweetness and enthusiasm for life would be here with us again.

We have all faced challenges in our life. Cynthia today faced one of hers and overcame it well.

We must always persevere, and today Cynthia truly did. Let's please give her a round of applause for a job well done."

As the class began to clap for Cynthia, Cynthia, who sat on the floor, again began to cry. But this time, she seemed to be laughing, choking, and smiling under her tears and the thunderous applause. A few students walked over and put their hand on her shoulder. Catharine gave her a hand, and they stood up and walked to the project table. Cynthia wiped the tears out of her eyes. Miss Maisie went back to her desk, and sat down, relieved that everyone seemed to be feeling better. It wasn't long before she encountered Cynthia one morning, and asking how she was, received a resounding, "Great!"

# CHAPTER 13

# LUCAS 2016

Lucas was a normal kid on the surface. He came to school everyday with his hair combed, his teeth brushed, and his clothes were always clean. He was one of Miss Maisie's most polite sixth grade boys. In a year when the boys were notoriously misbehaved, Lucas was always kind, considerate, and even joyful. There was one day Miss Maisie was out sick. When she got the report back from the substitute teacher, she was prepared for the absolute worst. And it wasn't the best—she learned that the sixth grade boys had decided to taunt one particularly shy young girl, in a lewdness only sixth grade boys can come up with. The taunting had been stopped by Lucas stepping into the scene and announcing that they needed to stop now, that, "This would never happen if Miss Maisie were here." Miss Maisie, at the end of the class day, pulled Lucas aside and thanked him for his bravery. Lucas stoically nodded. This was just who he was.

There was one place where Lucas did struggle. Sixth grade was a season of larger projects being assigned to students. Perhaps a visual history of Mesopotamia, or an introduction to the migratory patterns of a certain bird, with specific attention paid to the varieties of ecosystems they might thrive in. Most students relished the chance to do these larger scale projects, and so did Lucas, but he would become so massively overwhelmed by all he had to do, he almost never turned a project in on time, if at all. Miss Maisie was sympathetic when Lucas came in with a large piece of posterboard, and all he had on it was the title, "Galaxies, Universes, and Planets". He had also drawn Earth and Mars, and had printed out and pasted an image of a far away galaxy.

"I can't do it, Miss Maisie, I just can't do it." "What do you think the problem is?" asked Miss Maisie, her notoriously kind eyes putting Lucas at ease.

"I just don't know what to do, Miss Maisie."

"Well, let's take a look," said Miss Maisie.

Miss Maisie took the large poster board in her hands. "I love this drawing you did of our planet, Lucas. You really have talent as an artist."

"Thanks," said Lucas.

"So, let's start with what your overall plan was for this project. Can you tell me what you were thinking?" "What do you mean?" asked Lucas, "I was just trying to do the assignment."

"I understand," said Miss Maisie, "but sometimes, to get something like this done, which is a big project, we have to start one place and work backwards."

"I see," said Lucas. "Well, I wanted it to show information about each planet, and then how those planets fit into each other, and then into the galaxies, and then into the Universe."

"Right there, it sounds like you already know what you need to do!" exclaimed Miss Maisie.

"I just don't know where to start," said Lucas, in pain.

Miss Maisie took a blank sheet of printer paper. She handed it to Lucas. "On this sheet of paper," she said, "everything can come true." Lucas timidly shuffled the paper closer to him, and took out his favorite pen. "So, we are going to work backwards," said Miss Maisie. "Start with the end goal, and then we will break it into the steps that we need to get there."

Lucas wrote on the top of the page, "Image of the Universe". Then, Miss Maisie had him draw a line below it, and he broke it into sections, "galaxies, planets, comets".

"This looks great," said Miss Maisie. Miss Maisie then had him break the sections down further, until he had a detailed outline of everything he wanted to say about each section.

"Now look," said Miss Maisie, "It's like we've cut everything Lucas got home with his posterboard, to his small trailer where he lived with his mom. The ground was covered in a gigantic mess. His mom worked three jobs at minimum wage, which was enough for Lucas to always have nice clothes, but barely enough for them to get by. He cleared off a pizza box and some cartons of cigarettes from the makeshift dining room table, and set down his posterboard. He realized he forgot colored pencils at school.

"Mom," he asked, "can I go back to the store and get some colored pencils?"

His mom was on the phone in the other room, but she tucked the phone in her neck and looked in to see her son. "We really can't afford that right now, Lucas."

Lucas was crushed, but he resolved to do the project in regular pencil. He could always stay in at recess and do some coloring. Following his outline that he'd made with Miss Maisie, completing the project was a breeze. He enjoyed every minute of it. *I should have been doing this for forever,* he thought to himself.

Lucas heard his mom talking from the other room. "Lucas wants colored pencils, and I hate having to say no. I am just so overwhelmed with everything. I don't even have time to think about what I could do differently. No. No, I can't do that. I wish it would just be different."

Lucas listened to his mom, and he dropped his pencil. A feeling of sadness overcame him. He looked around at the disheveled home, and he thought about his mom. How much she loved him. How hard she worked. He looked at his neat little outline he had made with Miss Maisie, and then at the posterboard, which was quickly being filled with all kinds of wondrous images and interesting facts. If only what his mom had to do was also that simple.

Then, it dawned on him. He grabbed his outline and ran to his mom. "Mom, Mom!" he exclaimed.

"Hold on, Lorraine," said his mom. "Honey, one second." "Mom!" insisted Lucas.

His mom raised the phone back to her mouth, "One second; I'll call you back." "What is it honey?" asked his mom.

"Look at this," said Lucas, holding up the sheet of paper he'd been given by Miss Maisie.

Lucas's mom brought the paper to her nose, examining this outline that had something to do with the Universe.

"This is great, Lucas, very nice work. I'm glad you are learning so much," said his mom, a bit annoyed at this naïve interruption. "I am going to call Lorainne back, okay?" said his mom, reaching for the phone.

"No!" said Lucas, "Look! This can solve your problems."

Lucas's mom took a closer look at the paper. "Look," said Lucas, "just start with the place you want to get to, what you want the whole thing to look like when it's done, and then break it into little steps and work backward." Tears welled in his mom's eyes.

"Honey, that is so sweet," she was tearing up, "thank you."

"You're welcome," said Lucas, nonchalantly. "Now excuse me, I need to get back to work on my project."

"Sure thing," said his mom, "You do that. I will be here if you need anything." Lucas's mom stared down at the paper. She was taken aback and moved to think that perhaps there was something to her son's suggestion.

That night, as Lucas fell asleep, he could see his mom through the crack in the door, sitting at the table in front of a piece of paper.

"Thank you, Miss Maisie," he said to himself softly, before drifting off to sleep. As he awoke the next morning, he felt excited for the day. He felt excited for his project and to finish it at school. He felt excited for Miss Maisie, and he felt excited for his mom. The project got Lucas a good grade, and as the school year wore on, he got better and better at using outlines to organize all of his big ideas. On one particular day, Lucas was leaving class with a big grin.

"What are you so happy about?" asked Miss Maisie, humorously.

"I am going to the art store after school with my mom!" exclaimed Lucas.

"Wonderful," said Miss Maisie, "I will see you tomorrow! Bye Lucas." "Bye Miss Maisie," said Lucas, as he bounded out the door.

# CHAPTER 14

# MISS MAISIE 2020

Miss Maisie, who you by now know well, retired after thirty-five years of teaching. When she decided to retire, it was the year a global pandemic raged. All the businesses were shuttered, no one was gathering inside anywhere. Miss Maisie was shrouded in a heavy cloud. She had long dreamed of a retirement party where she would get to celebrate with the other teachers, and maybe even some of her former students might come! She was so eager to have this closure to her life with her children. The day she left her classroom for the last time, she closed the door and wept alone on her way to the parking lot.

Miss Maisie was among the most loved teachers that ever taught at Bluebonnet. She had taught generations of students, students who had grown up and become doctors, mothers, police officers, firemen, nurses, politicians, and grocery store owners. All kinds of varieties of happiness had found them. Miss Maisie sometimes wondered what, if any, role she had played in their life. She felt like she had done a good job with everything that had been asked of her over her long career, but today she couldn't think to muster the strength of what was being asked; to retire and bid her life of teaching goodbye. She looked at her school and her classrorom, and she remembered all of the memories that had happened in this small space.

Sure, she had moved from one grade to another. She had a 'floater' around the school and had been on different floors, often coming in to restore normalcy to a classroom. She had taught first grade and eighth grade and then first grade again. But wherever she went, wherever she landed, it was Miss Maisie's classroom. Now, she had to say goodbye to the place which had been her home. She knew the younger teachers had what it took to be the teachers they needed here at the school. She had personally helped mentor so many of them. But today was just a day of sadness.

Miss Maisie carried the last of her things out to her car. As she loaded the boxes into her trunk, she thought again about how great it would be for her to have a retirement party.

"Excuse me," she heard from behind her, "can I take a picture with the Bluebonnet sign here? I went here a long time ago and want to show my kids where I went to elementary and middle school."

And then, Miss Maisie heard a child's voice pipe up, "We want to meet Miss Maisie."

Their mom responded, "She has probably retired long ago, guys."

"I am Miss Maisie," said Maisie, turning around, tears welling in her eyes. "Who are you?"

"It's Ramona! Remember me?"

"Ramona!" she exclaimed, beginning to cry, "How could I ever forget?" They ran and embraced each other, casting aside the pandemic raging around them for a moment. "You look amazing, wow, and these are your kids?" asked Miss Maisie. "Hi guys, what grades are you in?"

The little boy piped up, "first" and the little girl piped up, "third". The little girl continued, "Mommy said that you are the reason she is a teacher."

"That is very sweet of her," said Miss Maisie. "Maybe I played some small part."

"Miss Maisie," said Ramona.

Maisie interrupted her, "Just Maisie, please."

Ramona blushed, "I don't know what your plans are this evening, but I and some of my old school friends are having a little backyard barbeque, around five. You should come over!"

"I would love to, dear," said Maisie.

At five p.m., Miss Maisie arrived at the retirement party of her dreams, orchestrated by something beyond her wildest imagination. There she was, at Ramona's parent's house, and the backyard was filled with people, at a safe distance, sharing stories of the good old days, many of which included the honored guest, the one and only, Miss Maisie. Miss Maisie enjoyed herself, and chatted with a number of her old students, laughing and crying the whole time. When the sun started to set, and a chill filled the air, Ramona proposed a toast.

"Here's to the one and only Miss Maisie, who today is celebrating 35 years of teaching and a Well-earned retirement!" began Ramona, as everyone clapped for her. "I want to remember what Miss Maisie taught me on my first day of school, to never be afraid to say hello, something that has opened countless doors in my life."

"I have a toast," a man said from the corner. "I want to thank Miss Maisie for always encouraging me to be the

leader I always knew deep down I could be. It has served me well in my life."

"Thank you, Reuben," said Maisie, warmly.

"If it weren't for Miss Maisie," a woman Maisie knew to be Adina said, raising her glass, "I never, ever would have been organized enough to go to college." Everyone laughed and cheered.

"I'll tell you what Miss Maisie taught me," said a voice Maisie still recognized as only belonging to Timothy. "If I treat my things well, they might stick around a little longer." Maisie smiled and saluted him.

There was one more girl, timidly in the corner stirring her soda, "Maisie," she said quietly, "If it weren't for you, I feel like the world would have trampled over me." This brought tears to Maisie's eyes, who walked over and gave her a hug.

Now it was Maisie's turn, "Class," she began, which brought a chuckle out of the party, "if it weren't for you, my life would have lacked so much meaning, and my destiny would have been so profoundly incomplete. So here's to all of you!"

And as they said their individual goodbyes that night, Miss Maisie was able to say goodbye to her years of dedication and teaching, and say hello to the legacy she left behind.

# BIOGRAPHY

Dr. Rudy Mendoza is a proud native Texan. During his early years he dedicated two years missionary service in Costa Rica, Central America where he developed a passion for teaching and serving others. Dr. Mendoza earned his bachelor's degree in Latin American Studies from Texas Christian University. Go frogs! He acquired his master's degree in Educational Leadership from the University of Texas at Arlington. While serving with distinction as an elementary principal, he was selected to attend the University of Texas at Austin where he completed doctoral studies in Educational Administration.

Dr. Mendoza is experienced in teaching a broad array of learners ranging from elementary to adult students. Additionally, he has extensive administrative experience at the campus and central office level serving as an Assistant Principal, Elementary and High School Principal, and Director of ESL. He has a consistent record of creating high-performing academic learning communities and supportive learning environments in working with at-risk student populations. His educational philosophy focuses on differentiated instruction through an effort-based, collaborative learning and critical inquiry.

He has achieved over 20 years of experience in education. He believes that focusing on one learner at a time and helping them develop their own personal path can change their stars. Because of Dr. Mendoza's desire to serve he mentors' teachers, offers educational consulting, and coaches at all levels for those who want to improve student outcomes.

Outside of work, he enjoys spending quality time with family and engaging in a variety of outdoor activities such as hiking, exploring, camping and cultural arts.

www.ingramcontent.com/pod-product-compliance
Lightning Source LLC
LaVergne TN
LVHW022002060526
838200LV00003B/63